Africa

Leila Merrell Foster

Heinemann Library
Chicago, Illinois

© 2001, 2006 Heinemann Library
a division of Reed Elsevier Inc.
Chicago, Illinois
Customer Service 888-454-2279
Visit our website at www.heinemannraintree.com

Designed by Joanna Hinton-Malivoire and Q2A Creative
Printed in China by South China Printing Company

10 09 08 07 06
10 9 8 7 6 5 4 3 2 1

New edition ISBN: 1-4034-8539-9 (hardcover)
                   1-4034-8547-X (paperback)

The Library of Congress has cataloged the first edition as follows:
Foster, Leila Merrell.
       Africa / Leila Merrell Foster.
              p. cm. – (Continents)
       Includes bibliographical references (p.) and index.
       ISBN 1-57572-446-4
       1. Africa–Juvenile literature. [1. Africa.] I. Title. II. Continents (Chicago, Ill.)
DT3 .F67 2001
960–dc21

00-011464

Acknowledgments
The publishers are grateful to the following for permission to reproduce copyright material:
Getty/Robert Harding World Imagery/Thorsten Milse p. 5; Earth Scenes/Frank Krahmer, p. 7; Tony Stone/Nicholas Parfitt, p.9; Tony Stone/Jeremy Walker, p.11; Bruce Coleman Inc./Brian Miller, p. 13; Animals Animals/Bruce Davidson, p. 14; Bruce Coleman, Inc./Nicholas DeVore III, p. 15; Earth Scenes/Zig Leszczynski, p. 16; Bruce Coleman, Inc./Lee Lyon, p. 17; Corbis/Arthur Thevena, p. 19; Bruce Coleman, Inc./Bob Burch, p. 21; Corbis/K.M. Westermann, p. 22; Corbis/AFP, p. 23; Photo Edit/Paul Conklin, p. 24; Bruce Coleman, Inc/John Shaw., p. 25; Tony Stone/Sylrain Grandadam, p. 27; Bruce Coleman, Inc./Norman Myers, p. 28; Animals Animals/Leen Van der Silk, p. 29.

Cover photograph of Africa, reproduced with permission of Science Photo Library/ Tom Van Sant, Geosphere Project/ Planetary Visions.

The publishers would like to thank Kathy Peltan, Keith Lye, and Nancy Harris for their assistance in the preparation of this book.

Every effort has been made to contact copyright holders of any material reproduced in this book. Any omissions will be rectified in subsequent printings if notice is given to the publisher.

Some words are shown in bold, **like this**. You can find out what they mean by looking in the glossary.

Contents

Where Is Africa?

A continent is a very large area of land. There are seven continents in the world. Africa is the second largest. The **Equator** crosses Africa. The Equator is an imaginary line around the center of Earth.

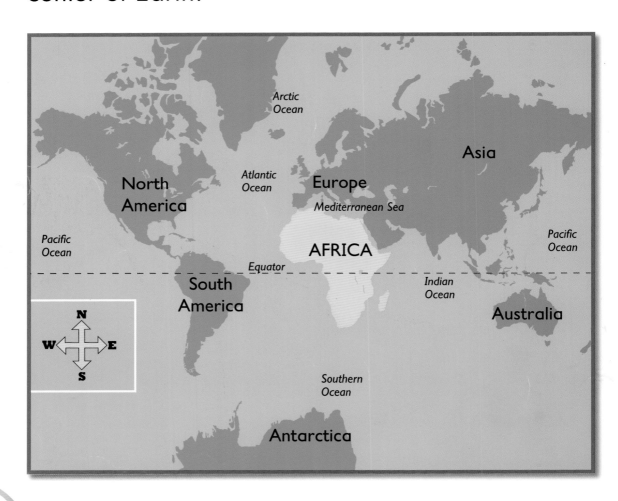

▲ *This is the Cape of Good Hope, in South Africa.*

Africa lies between two great oceans. The Atlantic Ocean is to the west. The Indian Ocean is to the east. The Mediterranean Sea separates Africa from southern Europe.

Weather

Because Africa is on the **Equator**, it gets very hot. There are **rain forests** in Africa. The **climate** there is hot and rainy all year round. In some parts of Africa, the highest mountains are covered with snow and ice.

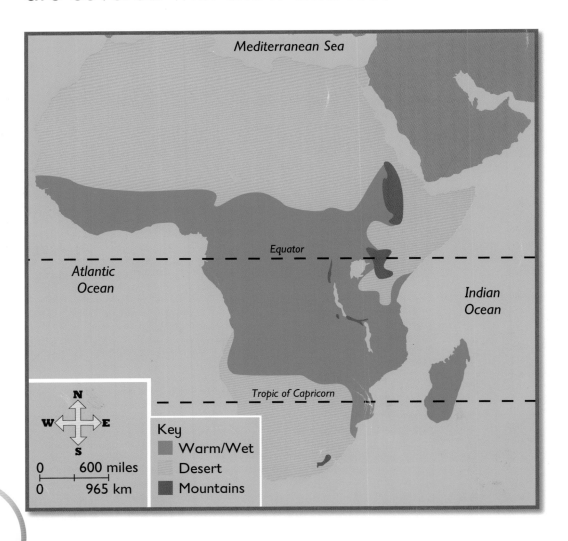

The Namib Desert has the highest sand dunes in the world.

▲ *The Namib Desert is in southern Africa.*

The **savannah** grasslands have a long dry **season** and a shorter wet season. It is hot all year in the huge **deserts**. At the southern tip of Africa, winter is warm and rainy. Summer is hot and dry.

Mountains and Deserts

Large parts of central and southern Africa are high and flat. The mountains in East Africa include Mount Kilimanjaro. It was once an **active volcano**, but now it is **extinct**. This means it no longer erupts.

Mount Kilimanjaro is the tallest mountain in Africa.

▲ *Mount Kilimanjaro is in East Africa.*

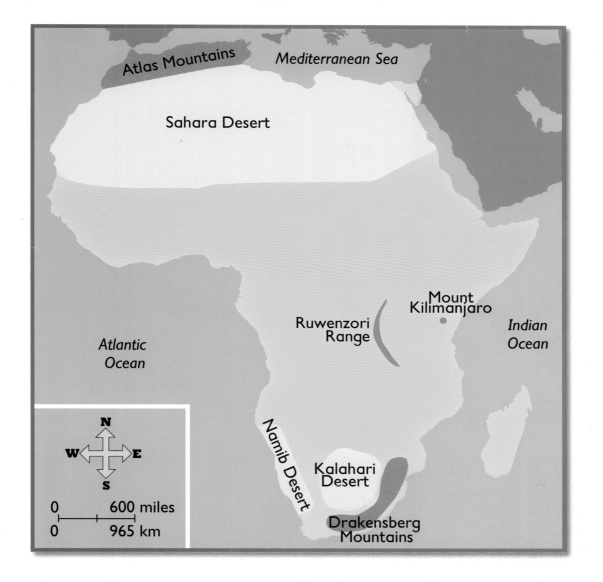

The Sahara **Desert** is the largest desert in the world. It covers nearly one-third of Africa. In the south, the Kalahari and Namib deserts are also huge. The hot African deserts have large sand dunes. They also have very hot winds.

Rivers

Africa has four of the world's greatest rivers.
They are the Nile, the Congo, the Niger, and
the Zambezi. The Nile River is the world's
longest river. It has many **dams** to hold
back water.

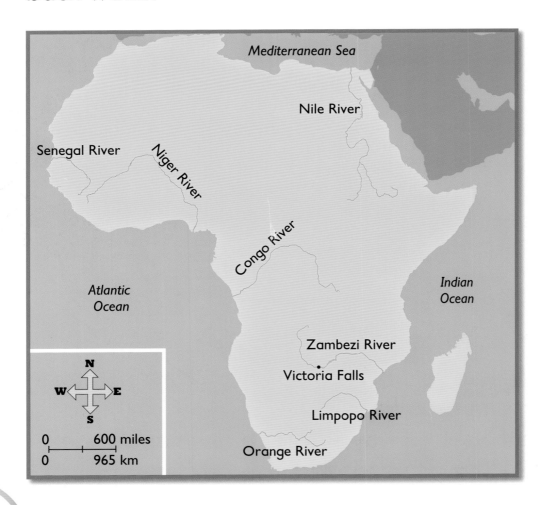

The African name for Victoria Falls is *Mosi-oa-Tunya*. It means "the smoke that thunders."

▲ *Victoria Falls are in Zimbabwe.*

The Zambezi River drops 355 feet (108 meters) into a rocky **gorge**. This is Victoria Falls. People can sometimes hear the roaring water 25 miles (40 kilometers) away. The falls were named after Queen Victoria, who was queen of England.

Lakes

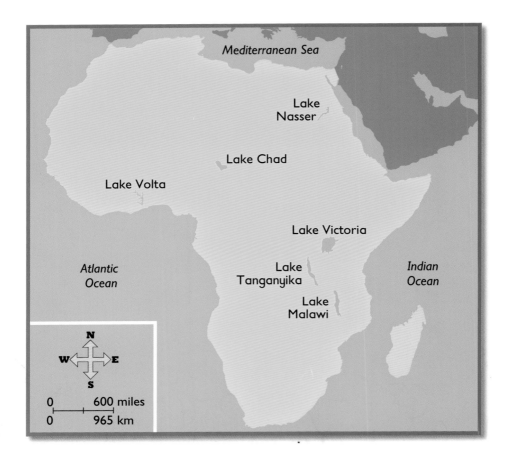

Africa has many lakes. Some lakes were made when people built **dams** on the rivers. Lakes Tanganyika and Malawi are in the Great Rift **Valley**. Millions of years ago, land slipped down huge cracks in the earth and made this valley.

Many people live near Lake Victoria and fish in its waters. But many fish are dying. Waste from factories and people has **polluted** the water.

Lake Victoria is one of the world's largest **freshwater** lakes.

▲ *Lake Victoria is in Uganda.*

Animals

Lions, elephants, and rhinoceroses all live on the grasslands known as **savannahs**. Zebras, wildebeest, and buffalo also live there. Giraffes eat leaves from trees. Eagles and vultures fly in the sky.

▲ *Elephants live in Kenya.*

Many African animals live in **national parks**, where they are safe from hunters.

▲ *This gorilla lives in Rwanda.*

Gorillas and chimpanzees swing through trees in the **rain forests** of central Africa. Crocodiles and hippos live in swamps. Flamingos and pelicans hunt for fish in rivers.

Plants

Thousands of plants and trees grow in the African **rain forests**. Some plants are very beautiful. Some are used to make medicines or food. People use the strong, hard wood from mahogany and ebony trees to make furniture and carvings.

▲ *These carvings are made from ebony.*

Thousands of years ago, the ancient Egyptians used papyrus to make paper.

▲ *Papyrus grows by the Nile.*

Papyrus **reeds** grow along the banks (sides) of the Nile River in Egypt. Palm trees grow in many parts of Africa. Some palms grow dates and some grow coconuts. Sometimes people use palm tree leaves to make roofs for their houses.

Languages

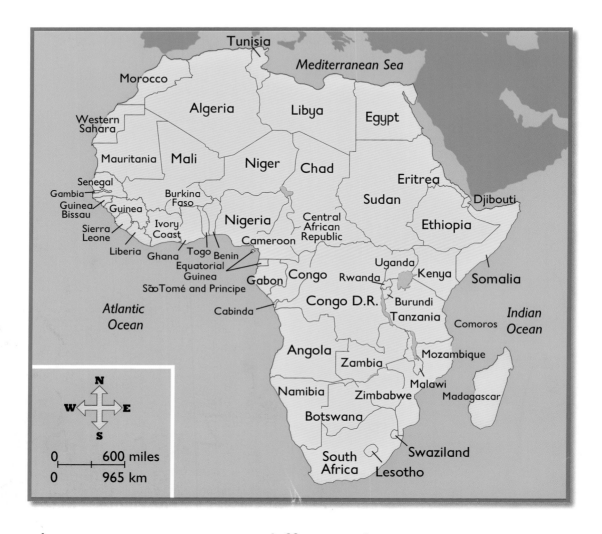

There are over 800 different languages in Africa. In the 19th century, many people from Europe came to live in Africa. Now, some Africans speak English or French.

In North Africa, most people speak Arabic. This is because hundreds of years ago, Arabs from the Middle East moved to Africa. In southern Africa, most people speak one of the many Bantu languages.

▲ *This is an Arab market in Egypt.*

Cities

This map shows some of Africa's most important cities. Johannesburg is the largest city in South Africa. It was built by Dutch **settlers** in the 1880s, after gold was discovered nearby. Gold is still **mined** there today.

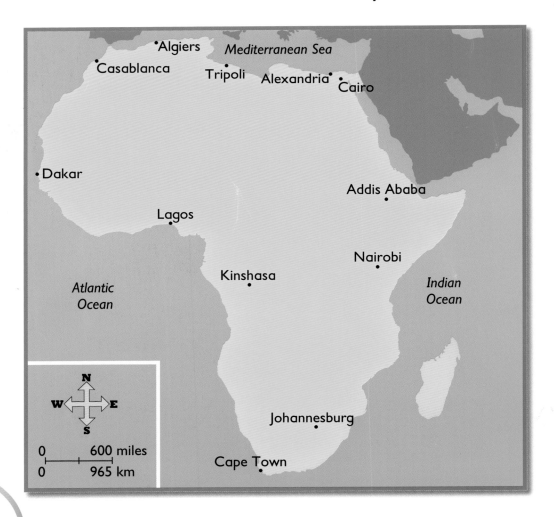

Cairo is the largest city in Africa. Six million people live there.

▲ Cairo is in Egypt.

Cairo is on the Nile River in North Africa. It is the **capital** of Egypt. Many tourists come to visit Cairo's museums. The museums contain amazing treasures found in the **tombs** of the ancient Egyptians.

The roof of the Hassan II Mosque can slide open.

▲ *Casablanca is in Morocco.*

Casablanca is one of the busiest **ports** in Africa. It has many modern buildings. The Hassann II **Mosque** is one of the largest mosques in the world. It is on a platform over the Atlantic Ocean.

Lagos, in Nigeria, is a busy port on the Atlantic Ocean. Many people are so poor they do not have proper homes. They live in **shacks** made from pieces of wood, metal, or cardboard.

Lagos is the world's most crowded city.

▲ Lagos is in Nigeria.

In the Country

Most people in Africa live in small villages. They grow their own food. Most villagers have farmed the same land for hundreds of years. In warm, wet areas of Africa, people grow bananas and **yams**. In the drier grasslands, many farmers grow wheat.

▲ *This village is in Guinea.*

Cattle **herders** keep moving to find new food and water for their animals.

▲ *These men herd cattle.*

Many Africans keep **herds** of cattle. The cattle produce milk. They are also sold for their meat. Some young Africans have moved to the cities to look for jobs in stores or factories.

Famous Places

The city of Timbuktu was an ancient **trading center** near the Niger River. It had a large palace, beautiful **mosques**, and a famous college. All the buildings were made of mud, so nothing is left of Timbuktu today.

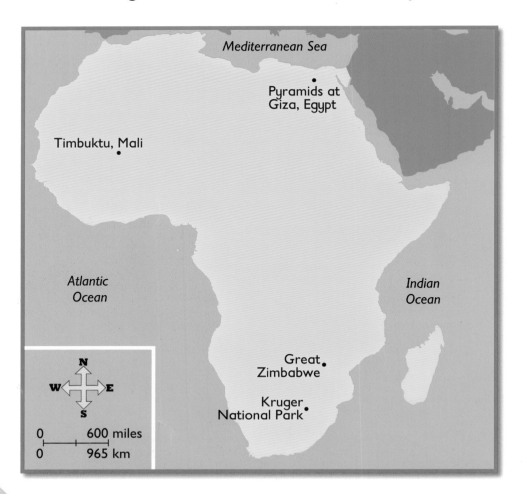

Mediterranean Sea

Pyramids at Giza, Egypt

Timbuktu, Mali

Atlantic Ocean

Indian Ocean

Great Zimbabwe

Kruger National Park

N
W   E
S

0   600 miles
0   965 km

▼ *These pyramids are at Giza, in Egypt.*

Thousands of years ago, the ancient Egyptians built a group of stone pyramids close to the Nile River in Egypt. The Egyptians buried their rulers, known as pharaohs, deep inside these pyramids.

Only a few walls of this great city remain.

▲ *This is what is left of Great Zimbabwe.*

About 1,000 years ago, people from all over southeast Africa began to bring gold to Great Zimbabwe. The rulers of Great Zimbabwe became rich and powerful. They built a great city out of stone.

The Kruger **National Park** was set up in 1898 to protect animals from hunters. People go on safari there. This means they travel around the park to see the lions, elephants, giraffes, and zebras.

The Kruger National Park is the biggest wildlife park in the world.

▲ *Kruger National Park is in South Africa.*

Fast Facts

Africa's highest mountains

Name of mountain	Height in feet	Height in meters	Country
Kilimanjaro	19,331	5,892	Tanzania
Mount Kenya	17,057	5,199	Kenya
Mawensi	16,893	5,149	Tanzania

Africa's longest rivers

Name of river	Length in miles	Length in Kilometers	Where in Africa	Sea it flows into
Nile	4,160	6,695	North/East Africa	Mediterranean Sea
Congo	2,781	4,373	Central Africa	Atlantic Ocean
Niger	2,590	4,167	Africa	Gulf of Guinea

Africa's record breakers

Africa has more countries than any other continent.

The Sahara **Desert** is the largest desert in the world. It is almost as big as the United States.

Lake Victoria is one of the world's largest **freshwater** lakes. It covers an area about the same size as West Virginia.

The island of Madagascar, off the east coast of Africa, has some animals that are not found anywhere else in the world.

The Kruger **National Park** is the biggest park for wildlife in the world. It covers over 7,700 square miles (20,000 square kilometers).

The highest temperature ever recorded was in Libya, in Africa, in 1922. It was 136.4 °F (58 °C) in the shade.

Glossary

active volcano hole in the earth from which hot, melted rock is thrown out

capital city where government leaders work

climate type of weather a place has

dam strong wall built across a river to hold back water

desert hot, dry place with very little rain

Equator imaginary circle around the exact middle of Earth

extinct no longer active

freshwater water that is not salty

gorge very deep river valley with steep, rocky sides

herd big group of animals

herder someone who looks after a group of animals

mine to dig up things from under Earth's surface

mosque building used for worship by Muslims

national park area of wild land protected by the government

polluted poisoned or damaged by something harmful

port town or city with a harbor, where ships come and go

rain forest thick forest that has heavy rain all year round

reed type of grass that grows near water

savannah grassy area with few trees, found in hot countries

season time of year

settlers people who come to live in a country

shack small, roughly built hut or house

tomb place where the dead are buried

trading center place where many things are bought and sold

valley low area between hills and mountains

yam sweet potato

More Books to Read

Lynch, Emma. *We're from Kenya*. Chicago: Heinemann Library, 2006.

Parker, Vic. *We're from Egypt*. Chicago: Heinemann Library, 2006.

Spilsbury, Louise and Richard. *Watching Lions in Africa*. Chicago: Heinemann Library, 2006.

Index